50 keywords for

A Separation with Heart

from Acceptance to Zero hour

S. B.

50 keywords for

A Separation with Heart

from Acceptance to Zero hour

Bibliographical information of the Deutsche Nationalbibliothek [German National Library]. The German National Library lists this publication in the Deutsche Nationalbibliografie [German National Bibliography]; detailed bibliographical data can be accessed on the internet at http://dnb.dnb.de.

Typesetting, cover design, production and publishing:
BoD – Books on Demand, Norderstedt

ISBN 978-3-7562-6510-7

It took me a while before I summoned the courage to undertake this book project. From a little distance, in terms of time, and with a view that was no longer so emotional as before, I found it possible to compare what had been wishful thinking just a few years ago with the experiences I had gained, to filter out the result and write it down. I knew that despite the separation we would always remain a family, we would always remain parents. And both I and my ex-husband had our clear ideas about how we wanted to lead our lives after the separation, together with the children. Not in a way tied to locations or objects, but from a purely emotional, familial and friendly point of view.

A separation usually involves at least one heartbreak and a lot of broken crockery. Two people have come together out of love, friendship, respect and confidence. They have experienced a lot together over the years, perhaps started a family and certainly have many wonderful memories. Sadly, all that is often forgotten far too quickly. Then only destruction remains, and a whole family and a whole lot of feelings are caught up in the train wreck. Especially when children are involved – no matter what age they are – this must not be allowed to happen! Every adult should consider what his or her goal is; yet more anger and grief, or just possibly, a constructive 'togetherness'? It is imperative to distinguish the couple level from the parent level. Even if you no longer have much sympathy for the father or mother of your children because you have been betrayed or hurt, that very person can still be a caring father or loving mother. It takes a lot of strength, patience and the power to walk the path ahead not out of revenge, but always with the aim of making the best possible use of the situation for everyone. I will try to make the path to this goal a little easier for you here, in these short, simply formulated chapters.

I dedicate this book to those who were hit the hardest by our separation: my two incredible children, who showed me that they can rise above themselves in the most difficult times. Then to my ex-husband, because without him we would not have been able to go through this time so constructively. My mother, who despite her advanced age has been an incredible support. She has such an understanding of the younger generation, I can take a huge leaf out of her book. And then all the rest of the family, as well as all the patient, tolerant and loving people who have accompanied me and us as a family on this path, and are still by our side today.

About me: I was born on 22 October 1964 in Zurich, and have lived on Lake Zurich for almost half my life. It was always clear to me that I wanted to work despite having children, and I am very happy about this decision today. The balance between family and career is ensured, and personal and financial independence helps you in all situations of life.

ACCEPTANCE

You are very clear about your family situation and your relationship, and you know that a separation is imminent or already in progress. You are also aware that it does you no good to fight against it. It robs you of energy and takes you off your path. Accepting your situation helps you to feel less pain and sadness. Acceptance does not mean resignation. You simply accept the situation as it is and try to make the best of it.

ACTION

You may be so full of grief and anger that you are unable to think clearly, let alone get anything done. You need to change that quickly, even if it's just by 'doing something'. This gives structure to your day. There are so many small and big things to do right now. Make a list of everything you need to clarify, organise and bring together: lawyer, budget, psychological support, self-care.

Take at least one thing each day that you can work through. The goal is to have one task and to finish it by the evening. You will be distracted during the day, but in the evening, you can cross something more off your list. Then when you go to bed, you know you don't have to worry about it the next day. But don't just focus on these tasks. Also make plans to go for long walks, or make an appointment with your hairdresser.

BLAME

Attributing blame – that sounds like 'pointing the finger' and not wanting to take responsibility. Who is to blame when a relationship ends? Can only one person be to blame? If you have been cheated on or a third person is the trigger for a break-up, then at first glance the other person carries the 'blame' for the whole situation. I can understand that very well. But instead of heaping blame on the other person, how about letting him or her speak? That takes some discipline and courage. You don't want your partner going into raptures about their new relationship, certainly. But how does he or she really feel about it? What events and feelings drew him or her into an affair in the first place? It is certainly incredibly difficult to sit across from your ex-partner in this situation and listen, without shouting and interrupting. But give it a try – it will certainly clear up the situation better in the medium term. And if both show mutual understanding and respect, this is a first, necessary step to avoid a very messy separation.

A big bravo and high praise goes to all those who are still able to meet each other amicably and with respect after a break-up. Be grateful for the beautiful moments in your relationship – they certainly did exist. Be grateful for your shared past and for the way you were able to develop because of and with each other.

Nobody thinks about a break-up or wants their partner to leave them. But it can happen, we all know that. If you can see something positive in it, despite the hurt, anger and sadness, and look to the future with confidence, then I say you deserve a round of applause!

BRAVO

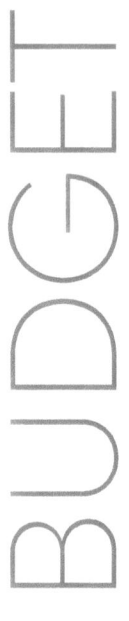

BUDGET

No matter what your financial situation is, make your own budget. For you alone, or for you and your children, cats, dogs, etc. based on your current life, including all hobbies and all outgoing expenses: petrol, food including pet food, electricity, holidays, cosmetics and clothes, reading, sport, telephone, all health insurance and other insurances, dental care... Simply everything. The best approach is to work through the invoices folder. If you haven't taken care of your finances in the past, now is the time to start. Go through each item and you will be shocked at what you can spend money on as a family. The point is, as long as the children stay with you, your expenses won't change much. That's why it's necessary to get an accurate overview.

Don't we humans generally have a hard time with change? And especially when you have the feeling (which may be wrong) that everything will be more difficult afterwards. At some point, I made it my goal no longer to see an upcoming change as an insurmountable obstacle, but rather as a challenge that would help me move forward. And that's why I wanted just to tackle and complete any task that came my way, no matter how unpleasant it was. And since I have had this attitude, so I can see the positive side of everything and not the dark, negative side. I am able to tackle tasks without anxiety and look forward to the changed situation.

CHILDREN

My children, or rather our children, are the best thing that has ever happened to me. The most precious. That's why it was extremely important for me not to harm these children's souls even more with a War of the Roses. I had a guilty conscience for a long time and wanted to give the two of them an intact family, but things turned out differently. It quickly became clear to us that we would wait to announce the separation until the children had reached a certain age, a certain point in their development and education. We still put our ego and our desire for separate ways on hold. Maybe this seems suboptimal from a psychological / educational point of view, but in our case it paid off – as our two grown-up children can testify today.

As soon as I had absolute clarity about my situation, about what I wanted (not about what I no longer wanted; big difference!), I came a long way in a short time. I no longer had to be constantly explaining and justifying myself for my ideas and actions. Because it was clear to everyone that I knew what I wanted and that I was on my way. You radiate something that 'disempowers' your partner. There is a certainty in your words that no one doubts any more. And even if emotions are involved, you still remain objective. What could be better for you than to bring a situation like this to the table, without angry discussions and tears? You are being authentic, just being perfectly clear!

COMPASSION

You definitely need compassion. There will be so many situations in this time of separation that you need to be able to empathise with. Compassion is the rationality that mediates between spontaneous, undistanced empathy and the coldly detached mind; between your feelings that overwhelm you, and your mind that makes you grow hard. Compassion can have a very positive effect and help your opposite number to cope better with the way things currently are. But you can only have compassion if you are at peace with yourself and the situation.

Yes, it takes courage to separate. You make a decision that you think is right despite the expected hurdles. A separation does not evoke positive associations. Hardly anyone will be happy with you about your decision. You will hear advice, concerns and warnings. It's meant nicely, but it's of little use to you. You alone have to walk this path and no one can take away even the smallest part of your pain, worries or fears. So, it is all the more important to prepare yourself, to act mindfully.

DILEMMA

Am I doing the right thing? If I separate? If I don't separate? Should I not wait for the children? Is it better if I draw the line for all of us now? Believe me, I was torn for months. And everyone out there sensed my insecurity and my dilemma. And everyone thought they had to be 'helpful' with their well-intentioned tips. You know exactly, you feel exactly when the time is right. And then you are ready to take the step into a new life. Don't let anyone distract you, because no one else walks the same path as you.

Distance in time and space heals. Even if it is difficult at first for one or both partners suddenly to find themselves really alone. Nevertheless, make a conscious effort to create a distance. If the children do not want this, declare your desire to be alone. Being alone has an incredible power. So many feelings come up, and you have time and space to look at them and process them. If you spend too much time together after a break-up, letting go becomes difficult. And that is what you ultimately want. When you gain distance, feelings – negative as well as positive – are put into perspective. And the possibility arises of establishing a healthy and, above all, neutral basis once again, as is desirable for you as parents;

EGOISM

How far does egoism extend, or in other words: where is the border between self-care and egoism? If the mother or father takes some time off after the separation to recharge their batteries, I think that's absolutely fine and very sensible. In the end, it helps everyone. But if the same people feel they need to catch up on the free life they have been missing out on, so they are only conspicuous by absence or unavailability, I find that a little bit problematic. It's not just about them, after all, there are usually other people involved in the situation. The children in particular are very dependent on a structured outcome. No matter what age, children need their parents, or at least one of them. They should have a place at home where someone familiar is there for them, and can help their troubled feelings to settle down again.

It's a feeling that everyone knows. People can actually be envious of your separation? Yes, they can. For all kinds of reasons. After all, you have had the courage to change your situation. You don't break down completely. You feel much better afterwards, physically and mentally. Your family still sticks together. You live a new freedom. It isn't exactly uplifting when you feel the envy of others. But what do they say? Envy is the highest form of admiration? Then take this thought with you and try not to pay too much attention to the envious.

FAMILY

The idea of writing this book only came to me because of the great importance that the family has for me. Two people decide to be together, start a family and will remain one until death do them part. The conventional traditional family is found less and less today. Nevertheless, whether living under one roof or separated, a family connects us and also obliges us in a certain sense. I see it as my responsibility to present my children with a family model that, even if not in the traditional form, can nevertheless work well for everyone involved.

You know this one, don't you? The fear of losing something, of no longer having something in your life. But just think about it for a moment – what is this 'something' exactly? Is it really the person with whom you have been together for many years, or is it all the background noise? The family structure, the familiar, the shared everyday life and perhaps too a whole lot of discussions and tensions? Yes, nothing will be the same after the separation and you have to get used to that. One kind of tension is gone, and what remains will initially be a vacuum. You suddenly have free time and a free mind. Discussions are no longer necessary, certain patterns and feelings no longer arise. An emptiness makes itself felt. When you deal with this emptiness intensively, which can hurt, you realise that the fear is unfounded. When something goes or has to go, something new and better comes along. Believe it. Use these moments of emptiness consciously, simply to do nothing or to visualise your new future.

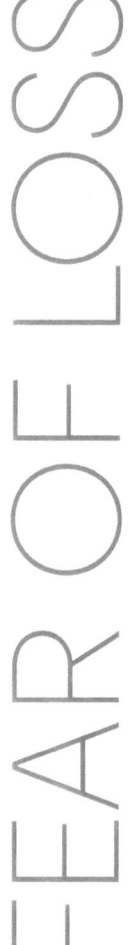

FEAR OF LOSS

FRIENDS

Friends come and go. The true friends stay, almost belong to the family, even after a separation. There are various reasons for this. Some simply can't cope with the situation; not everyone likes changes in life. I have noticed that some people couldn't handle our development because they would have had to deal with their own situation. Consequently, those people distanced themselves from one of us or from both. Understandable on the one hand, rarely a pity. It makes you wonder about the depth of the friendship. On the other hand, it is absolutely legitimate for friends consciously to choose one of the two separated partners. There are no conflicts of conscience and a friendship can still exist. But in any case, a lot of tolerance, forbearance and understanding is needed from all sides. Here, too, it is important to focus on oneself and one's immediate environment. The more you interact with too many people, the more confusion arises. Each of the two partners should be able to have their own circle of trust and support.

This keyword could have come right at the beginning. Paint a picture of your near future, your life after the separation. Visualise how you want to live, how the whole separation should go. What will your relationship be like, thereafter, with your ex-partner? Your children? Your family and friends? If you know this and know what you want to have in the future – not what you don't want any more, there's a big difference – then you are well on your way to achieving it.

GOOD ADVICE

Anyone and everyone out there will presume to give you any amount of advice, usually unsolicited. Be careful! Because in this situation you are often out of balance, and very grateful for any help that comes your way. Maybe you cry on your friends' shoulders and talk a lot with your family. All these people may really only want to help you, but they are also scared at the prospect of big changes in your life which will also make changes in theirs. And so they give you advice, even though no one knows your situation as well as you do or understands so well how you feel. So, these tips and well-intentioned advice can only lead to additional insecurity. If you want to get counselling, seek out a neutral professional whom you can trust.

Perhaps I should have put this at the beginning – as a keyword. But then some of you would not have read on; and without goodwill, you can forget about a separation with heart right away. It sounds difficult and almost impossible to do, but it is possible. I know it is. No matter what has happened, no matter how your story ended, meet your ex-partner with goodwill. If you absolutely can't do that, then meet the whole situation with goodwill. It is your story that needs to be resolved and you are in the middle of it. If you associate this whole story only with fear, chaos and hatred, then you are caught up in the midst of the chaos. You know what I mean?

GOODWILL

GRATITUDE

Gratitude is just one of those things. The word sounds so positive and yet there are many situations – there have been in my life – where I seriously asked myself what I had to be grateful for. Especially at times when you are stuck in a difficult situation. Or when everything around you threatens to collapse, and you have the feeling that your whole life needs to be reorganised. But actually, you have reason to be grateful every morning when you wake up. For your health, the roof over your head and your family. And the gratitude for the more difficult moments in your life you probably only feel in retrospect. Make a conscious effort to feel gratitude. You will see that there is something calming about it. You suddenly become aware of what you actually have and can put aside your anger about what you don't yet have, for a while at least. And when you increasingly practise highlighting what you do have, including what you have achieved with your family, some-thing very positive develops within you. Despite emotions, quarrels and a break-up, you have managed to set out on a new path. Yet another reason to be grateful!

Happiness means something different for each person. I am much happier since we separated. Although a separation demands an extreme amount from you – emotionally, administratively, financially – nothing remains the same as it was. But you alone are responsible for your happiness. And so you can also draw new happiness from a new phase in your life. Keep reminding yourself of what has improved with the new situation. What problems you don't have to deal with and will never have to deal with again. And keep your goal in mind: the happily separated mother and ex-wife. But also take a good look at your unhappy phases – you might still have quite a few of these to get through. Why are you unhappy now? What can you do to become happy (happier)? Listen to yourself, look at yourself, don't compare yourself with other people around you. Show the world, and especially yourself, that you can also become happy in a different way.

HARMONY

Nobody expects total harmony after a break-up and there is no such thing anyway. However, try to understand the behaviour of others. If that is not possible, accept what everyone thinks and does. The situation is difficult and everyone deals with it differently. You are now living as separated parents and have to keep the family boat afloat. This does not require harmony, but it does call for respectful relations and a lot of tolerance and patience.

HEALTH

Health is the highest good. Nothing in the world is of any use to you if you are not healthy. So pay attention to it. Especially in an exceptional situation like a phase of separation – and this is an exceptional situation – you have to take great care of yourself. Try to eat healthy food despite the grief that may be weighing on your stomach. Get out in the fresh air, even in the rain and snow. Exercise regularly; it clears your head and makes you feel good about your body, which in turn gives you self-confidence. Take vitamins and herbal remedies to support your body. Drink plenty of fresh tea and try to get plenty of sleep. If you can't get to sleep in the evening or wake up in the middle of the night with your heart racing, do breathing exercises or read a few pages of a book. Getting enough sleep is the most important thing. Your body needs to regenerate and you need to switch off for a few hours. And very important, but often very difficult: make times when the mobile phone is banned. This helps to prevent the noise in your head from getting louder!

HEART

That's just what this is all about. Even though it may have been broken, try to move on with an open heart. When your partner shows his worst side, show him and the world your best. Try not to stay stuck in the broken-hearted state, but move on. Picture where you want to get to – how this bad situation can change for the better for you and your family. Act from the heart and not from anger, resentment or hurt. This is the only way to get your partner to act from the heart as well.

You will often feel powerless and helpless as you go through the separation. This is normal. There will be situations where you feel no support, your children may turn against you and you feel in any case that no one understands you. Then focus on your goal and your task. You have decided to separate, that is your plan. You have a picture of your future in your mind's eye. Now look inside yourself – who or what is making you feel powerless? What statements or actions of others are causing you to lose your balance? Mentally go back to square 1, remind yourself of what you really want. Then you can overcome your helplessness.

HELPLESSNESS

Honesty is a cornerstone for me in a relationship. Probably because I'm once bitten, twice shy when it comes to dishonesty. I am also convinced that the more dishonest you are, the more dishonest people will flock around you. Honesty can also hurt, but in the long run you can only get ahead as an honest person. Making honest, clear and friendly announcements may cost a little effort, but it is incredibly liberating. What about when the children demand absolute honesty? You can't lie to them, but when it had to do with marriage and relationships, I didn't think it was necessary to give them an answer to everything. So I argued that certain topics were none of their business. On the whole they could handle that.

Probably some of you see me as a highly unrealistic idealist. I have had times when I could hardly trust anyone, not knowing whether the promise made to me this morning was still valid. I was sad, angry, desperate, at times I was at my wits' end. If we hadn't had children, I would have packed my bags and left. But because of the children, that was not an option for me. Back then I had said Yes to him and to our family, and my primary goal was to find the best solution for everyone involved. And today I can proudly say: we made it and we are all better off as a result.

INSULTS

It is all too easy to find yourself hurling insults when you are hurt and no longer know how to defend yourself. At best, your partner will then feel confirmed in what he or she is doing, seeing that you are no longer in control of yourself. Usually you regret shortly afterwards what you said and above all how you said it. The insults will recur, or else the other person will no longer feel like dealing with you and having a conversation. The only thing that helps is distance. So you can calm down again, take a deep breath and try to communicate constructively and without shouting. Just think about it – maybe you would like to know just WHY you have reached this point? But most importantly, are you sure you are interested in a good solution for all those involved or not? Here again, objectivity, clarity and calmness are the quickest ways to reach your goal. And if you can also prove to yourself that you don't have to lose your composure completely, even in this difficult situation, then you have already won.

Everyone is allowed to be a little bit jealous, but what does 'a little bit' mean? Where does it border on pathological jealousy? Why are you jealous? Jealousy can be one of the reasons for a relationship ending. But if you are jealous of your partner after the break-up, it can be very difficult. Try to find the cause of your jealousy. Try to focus entirely on yourself by distancing yourself. Don't compare your life with the new life of your ex-partner. And certainly don't compare yourself with his new partner, if he has one. There will always be a reason to be jealous. See to it that you are happy with the new situation and be grateful for the step you have taken. Because if you manage to do that, dissatisfaction, and so jealousy as well, will disappear.

LAWYER

Any mention of a lawyer may sound like you are getting into a War of the Roses, but it doesn't have to be like that. Since I don't know much about the law, I decided to go to a lawyer. I discussed the whole matter with her. She has many years of experience and told me what could happen, but didn't have to. I knew what I was legally entitled to, what I should pay attention to and what I was better off not doing. This got many of my questions and uncertainties out of the way early on. With this basis, you can find a good solution with your ex-partner that works for both of you. Because the more bitterly you fight for something you think you are entitled to, the more your partner is going to fight back. And that is definitely a bad way to go. I only saw my lawyer twice during the separation; that was all I needed.

When it comes to letting go, you will be severely tested. Letting go is of course something that accompanies you throughout your life. If you don't let go, you get stuck in the past and don't move on. I would say that letting go will be one of the most difficult issues in this separation process – especially if you didn't want to let go! But I also know that the better and faster you can let go, the quicker you will move forward with your family in the separation process. What does it depend on? You must have confidence in what comes next, in the unknown and the new. You have to be able to accept that nothing will ever be the same again, but everything will be better. You can take responsibility for this with your actions. Because only you can change your situation – and that is what you want, after all!

The love of a lifetime, the true love, the disappointed love... What is love? Today I see love quite differently than I did almost thirty years ago when I first met my ex-husband. No matter how you define love, always remember that you got together out of love, maybe got married and started a family. If you never forget this point, then I am convinced that you can also separate with love, or at least with heart, not with hate.

LYING

I know today that the more you lie to your partner, your children and therefore to yourself, the more liars you attract into your life. In the end, you sit on a big, nasty pile of lies, surrounded by liars. And getting out of it is extremely difficult. Think about what a small lie can cause: a guilty conscience, chaos in your head, uncertainties – what did I tell to whom, who knows what? And suddenly you find yourself in the midst of an unmanageable, painful chaos. That's why my advice to you is: don't get into lying in the first place.

MONEY

That blessed money... And yes, ultimately, money is the linchpin in a separation or divorce. The formerly joint cash has to be divided, no matter who contributed to the household with how much salary. One household suddenly becomes two and, depending on the claims of each, it can become expensive or very expensive for both. It is possible to find a fair and workable solution for everyone. Make your own budget and look at it together. What is the use of both of you trying to extract as much money as possible from each other's pockets? It just damages everybody. Everyone needs to be able to continue a life, possibly in a new place. Everyone must have their daily needs met and has a right to leisure time, sports and holidays. The extent to which you organise this has to be looked at. The more and the longer you fight about money, the more bitter and expensive the matter will become. And if someone says that money isn't everything – well, yes, that's true. But you still have to fill the fridge, pay for insurance and be able to afford the odd treat now and then.

Once you decide to start a family with your partner, and your children see the light of day, you have a lot of responsibility. You think you know how everything works. But in reality you have no idea. Unprecedented feelings develop. Perhaps insecurities or fears arise? You don't learn what it really means to become or to be a parent anywhere – you learn it 'on the job'. You are happy for your children and you suffer with them, it doesn't matter if they are three or thirty years old, or even older. Morally you feel responsible for them until death. And that is why it is of the utmost importance to be aware of this responsibility. Always.

PAST

Let the past rest in peace, they say. It's not that simple. But it is extremely important in the separation process. Because the less you get stuck in the past, the better you move forward – with the separation, with your further development and ultimately with your whole life. If you dream wistfully about the good times you had together, you will only be sad and this sadness will determine every day of your life. The same is true when you are angry with your ex-partner: your anger influences your decisions, is a barometer of mood for all involved and in the last resort the whole process stands and falls with you. Of course, it takes some strength to let go of the past. But holding grudges or dwelling on the past only harms yourself. So go into your new life strong and proud.

PICTURE

I'm sure you too had a picture once in your mind of how you imagined your life with your partner would be until the end of your days. Maybe with a family. Now that picture has fractured or has been completely destroyed. These things happen. But I also had a very clear picture of my time after the separation. I saw myself happy, liberated and relaxed. No permanent quarrels with my ex, no children in a destructive conflict of loyalties, ongoing relaxed contact with my family and his, with our friends and acquaintances. We always remain family and this separation must never destroy that. And today I can proudly say that we have all succeeded admirably in making this picture a reality.

PREPARATION

Well, if your partner tells you on New Year's morning, standing in the doorway with his bags packed, that he is leaving you for another person, then you hardly have time to prepare. But in the case where you or the two of you are considering a separation, it is indispensable to prepare for it. On the one hand, there are legal and financial matters to consider. Legal clarifications must be made and a budget must be set. On the other hand, there is the spatial division; who lives where with whom and how. Talk to each other, make notes, mind maps. Depending on their age, involve the children as well. Emotions may also have a place in this preparation. By planning together, you can work through a lot of issues and it will be easier to steer towards a peaceful but separated future.

Whatever the reasons that have led to your separation, try to treat your partner with respect, though it may be particularly difficult if you are being treated disrespectfully yourself. This point is always the top priority in a relationship, especially during a break-up. Once the relationship has reached a certain level of disrespect, there is no turning back. Decent and purposeful communication becomes impossible and a good separation even more so. And above all – and this is why I think this point is so important – as soon as you too fall into this disrespectful attitude, you lose touch with yourself. You become emotional, perhaps loud, you lose control of the situation, of yourself. Always try to keep your composure. Visualise it; keep your body taut, have your goal in mind and treat the other person in the way you would like to be treated.

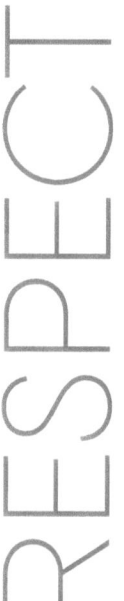

ROLE MODEL

As a parent, you want to be a role model for your children. And we know that is anything but easy. It's not so much what we tell our children, but what we act out for them. And it is in a situation that is sad and extremely wearing, above all, that you can show your children how you deal with it. The point here is not to model for the children the constantly happy family, but to teach them how to deal with conflicts in the event of a separation. It is sad enough to experience that the parents no longer live under the same roof. But it is all the more valuable to see that there are still many instructive and interesting facets between an all-out War of the Roses and the perfect family life.

Your life may be quite chaotic at the moment. And so you think you don't have time for self-care because you have to deal with all the organisation of your new life. Yes, it may be chaotic and you are emotionally so confused that you can hardly think straight. But that's why it's so important to take care of yourself. I don't mean holidays or wellness weekends, but a few minutes a day that are just yours. Meditate, do breathing exercises or go for a walk, take a bath or read a few pages of your favourite book. Try to dampen the noise in your head and reorganise your thoughts. It's important that there should be no disturbance from anyone: no phone, no WhatsApp, no children. So switch to airplane mode and close the door. If you manage to take a few minutes of time out every day, then you can already look forward to the following day and your oasis of time in the evening. You'll see, it works wonders.

SELF-PITY

Yes, of course, you feel you must be just about the most pitiable person on earth. No one loves you, no one understands you, no one has ever suffered such injustice. Let yourself fall into self-pity, bathe in it and be sad. But not for too long. It doesn't get you anywhere. It frustrates you and makes you even sadder. And above all, you focus on your problem and not on the solution. After one day of feeling really sorry for yourself, try to start the next day with a structure. This helps you to concentrate on your goal. You are diverted and do something for yourself, focus on the solution and appear much more self-confident. In this way, the spiral can begin to turn upwards once again.

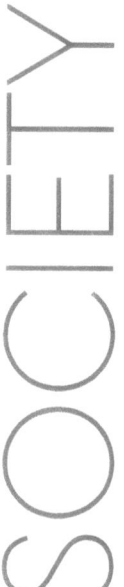

You might be inclined to think that in today's society the most diverse forms of living together are accepted. But as soon as you confront the people around you with the fact of your new way of life, you get little in the way of encouragement. Even though it is about you and not about them! Change is often very difficult to accept. That is why the most important thing is that you should be aware of your actions and have clear goals in mind. This is the only way to escape the voiced or silent criticism when you don't any longer move within social norms.

STRUCTURE

What you need now is a structure to get you through the day. Make a plan of what you want to achieve and by when. With all the tears, anger and upcoming changes, it's easy to get lost in your thoughts and only 'come back to yourself' when the sun goes down in the evening. And that is completely counterproductive. You want to develop further and cope with the new situation, you have a goal in mind. You have a picture of yourself and your new life in your head. And you can achieve this better with the help of a structured daily routine.

You will suffer from a separation, even if you have made this decision consciously. The mere fact that you are moving away from a former loved one, that a family is being torn apart and that nothing will ever be the same again, will throw you completely off balance. Counselling helps tremendously. Maybe you think, 'I can do this without external help'. Yes, you might, eventually. But an outside person (coach or therapist) points out things you can't or won't see from your perspective. This can trigger an avalanche of new insights. Supposedly insurmountable hurdles suddenly become surmountable or disappear altogether. Get the help you need. That way you will be speedier and healthier in reaching your goal.

SUPPORT

TOLERANCE

Tolerance is indispensable in the whole of life. But don't lose yourself in the process – and I know what I'm talking about. You can let someone be, as long as you stay with yourself. Listen to your inner self often, especially when you have a gut feeling, an uneasy feeling. Stop quickly and ask yourself: Am I really 'only' being tolerant, or am I already making concessions? Is it still right for me, do I feel comfortable with it? During my separation, my ego and my tolerance often clashed. Then I tried to find out which was stronger and which feeling I could trust. Most of the time it was because my ego had been hurt by previous incidents and I didn't want to be tolerant any more. But then I realised, after a certain amount of soul-searching, that being tolerant does not dent my ego but only helps me, and so also us, to move forward.

Don't make yourself the victim of a situation. As a victim you achieve nothing. You sink into self-pity and are unable to act. Even if your partner has left you, cheated on you or treated you badly, it always takes two to create a situation. Take responsibility for yourself and your actions, for the situation as a whole. Stand up, think, talk and act. This is the only way to get closer to your goal.

WALK

What you go through during a break-up – even before and after – is not a walk in the park. All the same, I think walks are brilliant; you are out in the fresh air and it clears your head. But the most valuable thing about a walk for me was the opportunity to have difficult but constructive conversations. Words are easier to find while walking, and you don't even have to look the other person directly in the eye. That's not unkind in this case, and it can be very useful. Just try it out!

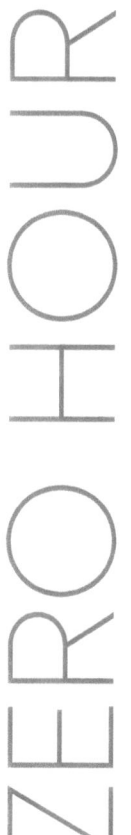

Is there a point in time when one should separate? Is it the right time, the wrong time, the best possible time? There certainly is no such thing as the right time. But I am convinced that by timing the whole process, you can limit the extent of the damage. Maybe you shouldn't announce the separation just before the children's final exams or on Christmas Day? Maybe you should discuss it as parents and put your own ego completely aside here (and hopefully not only here). You aren't obliged to be considerate of everyone and anyone, but when it comes to those who are most affected, you singly and you as parents have to include them in the whole process. Of course, this always requires that you and your partner can exchange ideas and behave accordingly. I don't mean that you have to act like a happy couple. But between that and constant conflict, there are many finer shades possible.

AFTERWORD

Actually, the most beautiful experience I have had while writing this book is the realisation that I really do live, or have lived, every single point as described here. I have living proof that it can work, that a break-up doesn't have to be a traumatic experience, but can be a valuable, instructive phase in your life. My wish for you is that you may find it the same!